AF575821

# Maine Coon

Bernard Conaghan

## TABLE OF CONTENTS



A Crabtree Seedlings Book

Crabtree Publishing
crabtreebooks.com

# School-to-Home Support for Caregivers and Teachers

This book helps children grow by letting them practice reading. Here are a few guiding questions to help the reader with building his or her comprehension skills. Possible answers appear here in red.

## Before Reading:

- What do I think this book is about?
    - *I think this book is about what Maine Coon cats look like.*
    - *I think this book is about how Maine Coons act.*
- What do I want to learn about this topic?
    - *I want to learn how Maine Coons act.*
    - *I want to know what Maine Coons look like.*

## During Reading:

- I wonder why...
    - *I wonder why their tails are long.*
    - *I wonder why their coats are long and shaggy.*
- What have I learned so far?
    - *I have learned some coats are one color.*
    - *I have learned some coats have a tortoiseshell pattern.*

## After Reading:

- What details did I learn about this topic?
    - *I learned their coats need daily brushing.*
    - *I learned their voices are soft and sweet.*
- Read the book again and look for the glossary words.
    - *I see the word **shed** on page 10 and the word **prey** on page 12. The other glossary words are found on pages 22 and 23.*

The Maine Coon is a top cat **breed**!

Its body is long and rectangular.

The Maine Coon's tail
is also long.

Its **coat** is long and shaggy. It feels silky and soft.

Photo
Fun Fact
The fur is shorter
on its shoulders.

Some Maine Coons
are one color.

Others have patterns such as **tortoiseshell** or tabby stripes.

Their coats need daily brushing. They **shed** a lot.

## Photo Fun Fact

Their fur can get tangled easily.

Exercise is important. These cats love to play **prey** games.

Maine Coons need to be fed carefully. They can become **overweight** easily.

## Fun Fact

Maine Coons love to swim and play in water!

Maine Coons are gentle and loving.

They meow a lot! The sound is called a **trill**.

Maine Coons make great pets. Would you like to **adopt** this top cat breed?

Are you ready to add a cat or kitten to your home? Answer "yes" or "no" to each question.

1. I have a lot of space for a cat.
2. I will feed my cat the right foods every day.
3. I will clean the litter box every day.
4. I will play with my cat daily.
5. I am ok if my things get ruined.
6. I will provide my cat with interesting toys.
7. I will not force my cat to do things.
8. I understand that not all cats like to snuggle.
9. I understand that all kittens grow up to be cats.
10. I will make sure my cat feels safe.

How many "yes" answers do you have?

**0–5:** You are definitely not ready to adopt. Maybe in a year or two.

**6–8:** You can start talking about adoption.

**9–10:** You understand how to be a responsible cat caregiver. You are ready to add a cat to your family.

# Cat Playtime

## Do

- Make play a daily habit.
- Use wand toys to keep your cat far away so you don't get scratched.
- Make toys from cardboard boxes with entry and exit holes.
- Play with each cat separately if you have more than one cat.
- Pull the "prey" away from the cat and not towards it.

## Don't

- Keep a toy in your hand and then tease your cat to get it.
- Encourage play with body parts, such as fingers.
- Place toys close to your cat's face.
- Frustrate your cat by only using laser pointers they can't catch.
- Punish a kitten or cat that scratches or bites during play.

# Glossary

**adopt** (uh-DOPT): To take a pet home and be its caregiver

**breed** (breed ): A particular type of animal within a group of animals

**coat** (koht): The natural fur or hair that covers an animal

**overweight** (oh-ver-WEYT): Weighing more than normal

**prey** (prey): An animal that another animal hunts for food

**shed** (shed): To cast off hair

**tortoiseshell** (TAWR-tuhs-shel): A pattern of two colors, such as yellow and black

**trill** (tril): A sound made by a cat that combines a meow and a purr

# Index



# About the Author

Bernard Conaghan lives in South Carolina with a German shepherd named Duke and a black-and-white rescue cat named Duchess. He is a coach on his son's football team. He always eats one scoop of peach ice cream after dinner.

Written by: Bernard Conaghan
Designed by: Jen Bowers
Series Development: James Earley
Proofreader: Kathy Middleton
Educational Consultant: Marie Lemke M.Ed.

Photographs: Shutterstock: Cover and throughout: ©2016 Ermolaev Alexander, © Nadya_Art, © Studio Ayutaka, © Net Vector, © ANNA_KOVA; p.3 frame © Denis Cristo; p.4 ©2023 Eric Isselee; p.5, 22 ©2015 Linn Currie; p.6, 22 ©2023 Miglena Pencheva; p.7 ©2017 Eric Isselee; p.7, 11, 15 ©2020 Lucia Fox; p.8 ©2021 nadia_if; p.9 ©2018 Andrew Will; p.10, 22 ©2022 Savvapanf Photo; p.11 ©2016 Olleg Visual Content; p.13, 22 ©2020 Nils Jacobi; p.15, 22 ©2017 Artbox; p.16 ©2020 OlesyaPogosskaya; p.17 ©2021 Nils Jacobi; p.18, 22 ©2020 Nils Jacobi

## Crabtree Publishing

crabtreebooks.com 800-387-7650



**Printed in Canada/012024/CP20231127**

**Published in Canada**
**Crabtree Publishing**
616 Welland Ave.
St. Catharines, Ontario
L2M 5V6

**Published in the United States**
**Crabtree Publishing**
347 Fifth Ave
Suite 1402-145
New York, New York 10016

**Library and Archives Canada Cataloguing in Publication**
Available at the Library and Archives Canada

**Library of Congress Cataloging-in-Publication Data**
Available at the Library of Congress

Hardcover: 978-1-0398-3846-8
Paperback: 978-1-0398-3931-1
Ebook (pdf): 978-1-0398-4013-3
Epub: 978-1-0398-4085-0